WAMPANOAG

Big Buddy Books
An Imprint of Abdo Publishing
abdopublishing.com

Katie Lajiness

abdopublishing.com

Published by Abdo Publishing, a division of ABDO, PO Box 398166, Minneapolis, Minnesota 55439.
Copyright © 2017 by Abdo Consulting Group, Inc. International copyrights reserved in all countries. No part
of this book may be reproduced in any form without written permission from the publisher. Big Buddy Books™
is a trademark and logo of Abdo Publishing.

Printed in the United States of America, North Mankato, Minnesota.
062016
092016

THIS BOOK CONTAINS
RECYCLED MATERIALS

Cover Photo: © NativeStock.com/AngelWynn; © iStockphoto.com.
Interior Photos: ASSOCIATED PRESS (pp. 13, 27, 30); © RosaIreneBetancourt 2/Alamy (p. 15); © NativeStock.com/
    AngelWynn (pp. 9, 11, 16, 17, 19, 21, 23, 29); Shutterstock.com (p. 26); © Lee Snider/Photo Images/Corbis (p. 25).

Quote on page 30 from CapeCod.com.

Coordinating Series Editor: Tamara L. Britton
Graphic Design: Adam Craven

Library of Congress Cataloging-in-Publication Data

Lajiness, Katie, author.
    Wampanoag / Katie Lajiness.
Minneapolis, MN : ABDO Publishing Company, 2017. | Series:
    Native Americans
LCCN 2015050498| ISBN 9781680782035 | ISBN 9781680774986 (ebook)
Wampanoag Indians--History--Juvenile literature. | Wampanoag
    Indians--Social life and customs--Juvenile literature.
LCC E99.W2 L34 2017 | DDC 974.4004/97348--dc23
LC record available at http://lccn.loc.gov/2015050498

CONTENTS

WAMPANOAG TERRITORY

Wampanoag homelands were in what is now the northeastern United States. They lived in present-day Massachusetts, Rhode Island, and nearby islands.

The people moved when the seasons changed. In summer, they lived near streams. In winter, they followed animals into wooded areas.

Did You Know?

The Wampanoag's native language is no longer spoken.

WAMPANOAG HOMELANDS

MASSACHUSETTS

RHODE ISLAND

CONNECTICUT

CANADA

UNITED STATES

MEXICO

N
W   E
S

7

HOME LIFE

Wampanoag homes were called wigwams. Many families shared one home. Inside, people used animal-skin blankets and made fires to stay warm.

The Wampanoag built wigwams with wood and covered them with bark or grass mats. Some wigwams were up to 100 feet (30 m) long!

WHAT THEY ATE

Growing crops, gathering food, fishing, and hunting were part of the Wampanoag's **customs**. Women grew corn, beans, and squash. And, they collected roots, wild fruits, and nuts. Men hunted birds and deer. They also fished in nearby waters.

Wampanoag women gathered strawberries, cranberries, and clams.

Daily Life

Wampanoag tribes lived in many villages. Each tribe had its own chief to serve as its leader. Every village had a sweathouse. Men and women used sweathouses to cleanse their bodies in cold weather.

The Wampanoag wore clothes made from animal skins. Both men and women wore leggings and moccasins. In cold weather, they wore coats made from rabbit or beaver skin. They crafted jewelry from shells and animal bones.

Women often sewed deerskin clothes for their family members.

In Wampanoag **culture**, everyone had a job to do. Men hunted and fished. Women collected food and did most of the farming. Children did not attend school. Instead, they learned new skills from adults.

Wampanoag women used animal jaw bones to shuck corn.

15

Made by Hand

The Wampanoag made many objects by hand. They often used natural materials. These arts and crafts added beauty to everyday life.

Colorful Weavings
Women twisted dyed plant fibers into ropes. Then they wove these ropes to make bags and sleeping mats.

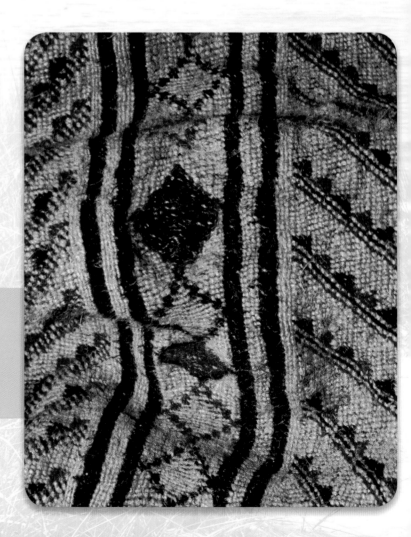

Stone Tools

A stone adze is similar to an ax. Men made boats by shaping logs with adzes.

Pottery

Women made clay pots to hold food or water.

Spirit Life

Each village had a faith leader known as a medicine man. This healer offered **spiritual** advice.

The Wampanoag held **ceremonies** to honor their native **customs** and beliefs. The people believed in a god known as the Great Spirit.

The Wampanoag saw a living spirit in everything around them. And, they thought everything in the world was connected.

The Wampanoag held a ceremony called Fire on the Water. At this event, they sat in boats while holding burning sticks. This tradition honored the earth, air, water, and fire.

STORYTELLERS

The Wampanoag tell stories to explain their **culture** and history. *Moshup* (MAH-shawp) is a common character in their stories. This giant eats whole whales in one bite. The Wampanoag believe his footsteps created the islands off the coast of Massachusetts.

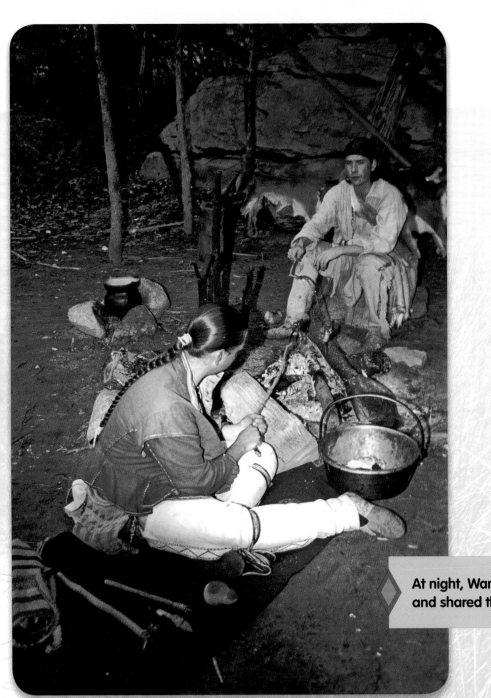

At night, Wampanoag sat around a bonfire and shared their native stories.

FIGHTING FOR LAND

The Wampanoag were a peaceful people. In 1620, they met British settlers. Chief Massasoit (ma-suh-SOYT) signed a **treaty** with the settlers that lasted 40 years. When he died in 1661, some settlers stole tribal land.

In 1662, Massasoit's second son became chief. The British gave Chief Metacom the name King Philip. He brought many tribes together to fight the British in King Philip's War. Sadly, King Philip and many Native Americans died during the war.

Metacom understood losing land threatened the Wampanoag's independence. He was a fearless leader.

After King Philip's War, the Wampanoag lost their land. So, they traveled to Nantucket Island and Martha's Vineyard, Massachusetts. Many Wampanoag adopted **Christianity** and new European **customs**.

The Wampanoag were a free people until 1788. Then the state of Massachusetts took control of the tribe. In 1907, the tribe lost its **reservation** on Cape Cod.

In 1684, the Old Indian Meeting House was built on Cape Cod. It was used to teach Native Americans about Christianity.

25

BACK IN TIME

1621

The Wampanoag and the settlers met for the first Thanksgiving meal. They gathered to honor the harvest.

Early 1600s

Most of the Wampanoag died from sicknesses brought by the Europeans.

1792

Only 20 Wampanoag still lived on Nantucket Island. The others had died from sickness.

1842

The state of Massachusetts separated native lands and then gave them out to individual tribes.

1972

The Mashpee Wampanoag Tribal Council was established. This council makes laws and has a tribal court.

1997

The Mashpee Wampanoag Indian Museum was established. Visitors can see **traditional** homes and how the tribes lived.

THE WAMPANOAG TODAY

The Wampanoag have a long, rich history. They are remembered for the first Thanksgiving meal with settlers and their tribal stories.

Wampanoag roots run deep. Today, the people have kept alive those special things that make them Wampanoag. Even though times have changed, many people carry the **traditions**, stories, and memories of the past into the present.

Did You Know?

Today, there are about 4,500 Wampanoag in the United States.

 The Wampanoag share their culture at events such as powwows.

"… the land belongs to everybody and no one…. I've always looked at the land as a gift from the creator to use and pass on to **generations** but to never own it."

– Chief Vernon "Silent Drum" Lopez of the Mashpee Wampanoag Tribe

GLOSSARY

ceremony a formal event on a special occasion.

Christianity (krihs-chee-A-nuh-tee) a religion that follows the teachings of Jesus Christ. Christians are people who practice Christianity.

culture (KUHL-chuhr) the arts, beliefs, and ways of life of a group of people.

custom a practice that has been around a long time and is common to a group or a place.

generation (jeh-nuh-RAY-shuhn) a single step in the history of a family.

reservation (reh-zuhr-VAY-shuhn) a piece of land set aside by the government for Native Americans to live on.

spiritual (SPIHR-ih-chuh-wuhl) of or relating to the spirit or soul instead of physical things.

tradition (truh-DIH-shuhn) a belief, a custom, or a story handed down from older people to younger people.

treaty an agreement made between two or more groups.

WEBSITES

To learn more about Native Americans, visit **booklinks.abdopublishing.com**. These links are routinely monitored and updated to provide the most current information available.

INDEX